THE NORMANDY LANDINGS

D-Day and Operation Overlord:
The First Step to Liberation

Written by Mélanie Mettra

In collaboration with Antoine Baudry
and Guillaume Henn

Translated by Carly Probert

History 50MINUTES.com

THE NORMANDY LANDINGS

KEY INFORMATION

- **When:** 6 June 1944
- **Where:** On the Normandy coast of the English Channel (Calvados and Cotentin)
- **Context:** World War II (1939-1945)
- **Belligerents:** The Allies against the Third Reich
- **Commanders and leaders:**
    - Bernard Law Montgomery, British General (1887-1976)
    - Dwight David Eisenhower, U.S. General (1890-1969)
    - Gerd von Rundstedt, German Marshal (1875-1953)
    - Erwin Rommel, German Marshal (1891-1944)
- **Outcome:** Allied victory
- **Victims:**
    - Allied camp: approximately 10 000 dead, wounded, missing or taken prisoner
    - German camp: approximately 4 000 dead and 6 000 wounded

INTRODUCTION

On 6 June 1944, from 6am, the Allied forces, mainly composed of American, British and Canadian troops, carried on ships along with weapons and tanks, landed on the beaches of Normandy. 'Neptune' was the first stage of Operation Overlord, designed to defeat the Third Reich of Adolf Hitler (1889-1945). Since the Battle of Britain (August-October 1940) and the armistice signed by France in 1940, the major scenes of conflict between the *Wehrmacht* (German army) and the Allied troops moved away from Western Europe towards Eastern Europe and Africa. After three years of German victories, the British and the Russians, initially supported by and then joined by the Americans at the end of 1941, progressed to the heart of the European fortress through a series of landings. After taking over North Africa, then a part of Italy, the Allies were now targeting the French coast to liberate the occupied territories and penetrate into Germany. The landing of 6 June 1944 set in motion the final, decisive phase of World War II.

POLITICAL AND SOCIAL CONTEXT

A GLOBAL CONFLICT

The landing of 6 June 1944 was both the first stage of a large-scale operation to undermine the German troops and liberate the occupied territories, and the completion of a strategy implemented several years previously.

After a blitz campaign began on 10 May 1940, Marshal Philippe Pétain (1856-1951) signed an armistice with Germany on behalf of France on 22 June.

However, the Allies continued to fight against Germany, and Britain obtained help from the USSR to complete its goal. Both countries benefitted from the "lend-lease" law, initiated by Franklin Delano Roosevelt (1882-1945), who was then President of the United States, and which was passed by the Congress in March 1941, aiming to support them materially while preserving U.S. protectionism. But the attack on the naval base at Pearl Harbor on 7 December 1941, by the Japanese forces, pushed the U.S. to take an active part in the war. While the Americans were fighting in the Pacific, the Russians were facing the German troops on the Eastern Front, in Crimea, Caucasus, and the British troops faced the *Afrikakorps* of the General Erwin Rommel in North Africa. The Axis forces maintained power over the Allies until the fall of 1942, when the situation took a decided turn.

The Rome-Berlin Axis was an alliance created on 23 October 1936, between Germany and Italy. Four years later, the act of the tripartite – which saw the creation of the Berlin-Rome-Tokyo Axis – was signed. Through this treaty, the countries involved recognized the domination of:

- Germany over Europe;
- Italy over the Mediterranean;
- Japan over the Pacific and East Asia.

To face the growing threat exerted by these totalitarian countries, many states came together to form what was known as the "Allies". In particular, this involved the United States, the Soviet Union and Great Britain – nicknamed the "Big Three" – and the Free France from 18 June 1940, Belgium, the Commonwealth countries (Australia, Canada and New Zealand) and the British colonies, Norway, the Netherlands, Poland, Yugoslavia and China. These countries demonstrated solidarity and implemented major joint operations involving several countries, unlike Germany, Italy and Japan.

In Africa, General Bernard Law Montgomery emerged victorious from El Alamein (Egypt, October-November 1942) against the German Erwin Rommel. In Eastern Europe, the sixth German Army of Friedrich Paulus (German Marshal, 1890-1957) capitulated in Stalingrad (February 1943) and the Red Army troops began their inexorable march towards

Germany.

In addition, the American industry accomplished a lightning-fast conversion to the production of war weapons, thereby strengthening the Allied position in the naval battles of the Atlantic and the Pacific.

In Italy, the U.S. landing on 10 July 1943 marked the fall of Benito Mussolini (Italian statesman, 1883-1945) and the signing of an armistice between the new Italian government and the Allies (3 September 1943).

Despite these various setbacks, the power of resistance of the German army maintained the extreme tension of the conflict and the outcome remained uncertain. It was becoming increasingly urgent for Allied leaders to find a decisive strategy, which led to the foundations of Operation Overlord being laid at the Teheran Conference (November-December 1943).

A PERIPHERAL ATTACK STRATEGY

From 1942, the British, Americans and Russians agreed on the need to multiply fronts to thwart the aims of Adolf Hitler, weaken the *Wehrmacht* and relieve the Red Army of the German pressure on the Eastern Front. Although Winston Churchill (1874-1965), British Prime Minister, wished to focus on the Balkans and North Africa – in line with his own strategic interests, including the Suez Canal -, he accepted, as a pledge of good faith towards his U.S. and Russian Allies, an intervention in Western Europe.

A first landing therefore took place in France, in Dieppe, on 19 August 1942. Operation Jubilee was conducted primarily by the Canadian troops who lost nearly a quarter of their men, and was a defeat for the Allies. The strategy that involved harassing the *Wehrmacht* in various points of conflict was nonetheless maintained. On 8 November 1942, the U.S.-British troops, supported locally by the French Resistance, landed in Morocco and Algeria, French territories defended by the armies of the Third Reich and the Vichy Regime. Operation Torch allowed the Allies to gain a foothold in North Africa and defeat the troops of Erwin Rommel.

Two months later, Winston Churchill and Franklin D. Roosevelt agreed on new landings, this time in Western Europe, at the Casablanca Conference (13-24 January 1943), from which Joseph Stalin (Soviet statesman, 1878-1953) was absent. Their first target was Sicily, aiming for Benito Mussolini's Italy. Therefore, on 10 July 1943, Operation Husky launched the Italian campaign which was ended by the Armistice of Cassibile on 3 September, between the Italians and the Allies. This did not cause the Germans to depart, and they continued to defend Italy, constantly pushing the Allies back until the end of the conflict.

To defeat the *Wehrmacht*, the Allies now needed to demolish Fortress Europe whose main defense was the Atlantic Wall.

GOOD TO KNOW

The Atlantic Wall was a defense set up in 1941 by the

Germans on the coasts of Norway, Denmark, Germany, the Netherlands, Belgium and France. The main ports were turned into fortresses and tens of thousands of fortifications (small bunkers, artillery, etc.) were scattered along the coast.

Inland, Erwin Rommel drowned the lowlands and set up his famous "asparaguses", which were wooden stakes planted in the ground to prevent landings of gliders and parachute drops. He would also have liked to have armored tank divisions near the beaches, to immediately repel any attempts at landing, while Marshal Gerd von Runstedt preferred to position them at the back to repel the Allies within the territory during an armored counter-attack. As this controversy could not be resolved, three divisions were stationed near the coast, while the rest remained in the land. However, none of these divisions could be moved without the consent of Adolf Hitler, which would later create many problems.

PREPARATIONS FOR OPERATION OVERLORD

Operation Overlord was part of this wider strategy of landings and penetrating the crucial points of the African and European territories. After four years of conflict, it was no longer enough to attack the German army from the outside to weaken them, and the Allies needed to change to a frontal attack.

At the Casablanca Conference, Winston Churchill and

Franklin D. Roosevelt lay the groundwork for a major operation in France. The COSSAC (Chief of Staff to the Supreme Allied Commander) was created and directed, under the leadership of British General Frederick E. Morgan (1894-1967), to schedule the operation for the spring of 1944. Under the code name 'Overlord', the operation was to take place in two stages:

- The first phase was Operation Neptune, which scheduled the landing of troops and material by sea, and the deployment of men by air – this was the attack phase;
- The second phase consisted of consolidating the bridgehead created and repelling the German army within the territories – this was the Battle of Normandy.

The Normandy beaches were chosen as a landing place, with the British coast as a base, for several reasons:

- fortifications there were less important;
- the Germans did not expect to be attacked on this territory which was so far from the heart of Germany.

The coast between the Cotentin peninsula and Le Havre port was divided into two areas: one was allocated to the U.S. Western Task Force, the second to the Anglo-Canadian Eastern Task Force. Five beaches were selected to conduct amphibious operations: Utah and Omaha were assigned to the U.S. troops; Gold, Juno and Sword were chosen for the British and Canadian troops.

From 28 November to 2 December 1943, during the Tehran Conference which brought together the three Allied leaders for the first time, Joseph Stalin validated the U.S.-British project, preferring it to the British proposition to land in the Balkans and in Italy.

On 6 December 1943, the SHEAF (Supreme Headquarters Allied Expeditionary Force), commanded by American General Dwight D. Eisenhower, replaced COSSAC and completed preparations for Operation Overlord.

The plan of attack was organized around three main objectives. First, the troops had to undergo intensive training. The exercises were held in Britain on beaches selected due to their similarities with those of Normandy (Slapton Sands, Culbin Sands, etc.). The last repetition (Operation Exercise Tiger) took place between 3 and 9 May 1944.

GOOD TO KNOW

During training, German submarines coming from Cherbourg and patrolling the Channel met the LSTs (Landing Ship Tank) carrying men from the 4th U.S. Infantry Division and the 7th Corps of the U.S. Army, who were due to land on Slapton Sands beach. The outcome was devastating: more than 600 men were killed and three LSTs were destroyed, jeopardizing the striking force of the Allies on D-Day.

The construction of artificial ports destined to receive the supply of men, equipment and fuel for the second phase of the operation was launched in the Thames Estuary.

Finally, at the same time, it was necessary to distract the enemy through a policy of massive disinformation. General Erwin Rommel, head of the German troops of Army Group B responsible for defending the Channel coast from January 1944, expected a landing, but did not know where it would take place. Operation Fortitude was deployed to convince him that it would occur in the Pas-de-Calais, near the English coast. This vast misinformation campaign led by Colonel John Bevan (1894-1978) was based on the desire to convince the enemy that the Normandy landings were a diversion to mask a larger scale operation that would take place in the Pas-de-Calais. To do this, John Bevan used all kinds of tricks, from the circulation of false information, to the creation of a ghost army on fictitious training grounds, to the use of inflatable tanks exposed to the view of the Germans reconnaissance aircraft. His efforts were rewarded: indeed, the German army focused on the coasts of the Pas-de-Calais.

On 1 June, the British radio station BBC broadcast the first message launching Operation Overlord to warn the French Resistance of the impending attack: the message consisted of the first verse ("With long sobs / the violin-throbs / of autumn wound / my heart with languorous / and monotonous sound") of the famous poem by Paul Verlaine (1844-1896), entitled *Autumn Song* (1866).

COMMANDERS AND LEADERS

DWIGHT DAVID EISENHOWER, AMERICAN GENERAL

Born on 14 October 1890, Dwight D. Eisenhower originated from Texas. He grew up in a very modest family and in 1911 he enrolled at the Military Academy at West Point. He was deployed during the First World War (1914-1918) in the tank training centers. Noticed by General George Marshall (1880-1959), he was called by him to the General Staff of Washington in December 1941, just after the attack on the American base of Pearl Harbor by the Japanese. He quickly became Deputy Chief of the operations to defeat the German troops and recapture Europe. Far from being a mere strategist, he took part in the operations he planned and played an important role as mediator between the British and American military leaders, thanks to his diplomatic skills. He led the landing in North Africa in November 1942, then those of Sicily and Italy from May to September 1943. At the end of November 1943, he left the Mediterranean to settle in London as head of the Allied Forces in Europe. As head of SHEAF, he participated in developing Operation Overlord, and in particular the planning of the actual landing. Once again, he was required to mediate between the Generals involved in the operation, the British Bernard Law Montgomery, the American George Patton (1885-1945) and the French Charles de Gaulle (1890-1970). Originally scheduled for 5 June, the landing was postponed by one day due to bad weather.

The success of his work led him to lead the NATO forces after the conflict ended. In addition, he ran for U.S. presidency in 1952. He won the election and renewed his mandate four years later. His legislature was marked by his usual diplomacy, particularly in relations between the United States and the USSR during the Cold War (1945-1990). He died on 28 March 1969.

BERNARD LAW MONTGOMERY, BRITISH GENERAL

A British officer born on 17 November 1887 to a pastor father, Bernard Law Montgomery was trained in weaponry at the military school of Sandhurst and took part in the First World War on the French Front, where he was seriously wounded. Appointed General in 1937, he commanded the 3rd British Division during the campaign in France. Posted in North Africa, his first confrontation with the German Marshal Erwin Rommel took place in 1942 in Libya, where he was first held in check by the troops of the *Afrikakorps*. He got his revenge at the Battle of El Alamein in Egypt. After the Allied victory in North Africa, he joined Dwight D. Eisenhower first in Sicily, then in London, where he collaborated with the American General for the implementation of Operation Overlord. He directed the land forces throughout the Battle of Normandy, despite his stormy relationship with Dwight D. Eisenhower. He then participated in the conquest of Germany, where, after the war, he commanded the British occupation troops between 1945 and 1946. He retired in 1958, after having been deputy commander of the NATO forces. He died on 24 March 1976.

ERWIN ROMMEL, GERMAN MARSHAL

Born on 15 November 1891 in Germany, Erwin Rommel became a lieutenant in 1912. Awarded the Order of Merit following his exploits during World War I, he remained in the *Reichswehr* (German armed forces authorized by the Treaty of Versailles) as an instructor in various military academies. He soon became very attracted to the natio-nal-socialist ideology of Adolf Hitler. He joined Hitler's party and was successively put in charge of the personal guard of the Führer and the training of the Hitler Youth. He was then appointed General by the Chancellor in August 1939 and followed him in the Polish campaign (September-October 1939) before being placed at the head of the 7th *Panzerdivision* (armored division). He was the first to enter France, crossing the Meuse with his tanks and then racing towards the Channel.

In February 1941, he was appointed commander of the *Afrikakorps* and won decisive victories over the British troops, which earned him the nickname "Desert Fox" and the rank of field marshal. Recalled by Adolf Hitler before the Allied victory in North Africa, he led the German forces in Italy before being charged with an inspection mission of the Atlantic Wall in the fall of 1943. In January, he took com-mand of army Group B, which included all of the German forces based between the Netherlands and the Loire whose mission was to protect the coast of the Channel. Aware of the imminent U.S.-British operation in that territory, he strengthened the defenses of the Atlantic Wall by installing new batteries, planting mines on the beaches, flooding plains and building forests of stakes behind the coasts.

On 6 June 1944, convinced that the bad weather would prevent a landing attempt, he went to Germany and received a message informing him of the arrival of the Allied troops while at his wife's birthday party. He immediately headed for France, where he was unable to contain the Allied advance. Already convinced, like other German officers, that the Third Reich was no longer able to win the war and that peace must be negotiated, he participated in the preparation of the plot against Adolf Hitler, who was opposed to any surrender. Rommel was arrested for treason, but the Führer waived his trial due to his popularity. However, he ordered him to poison himself, which Erwin Rommel agreed to do. He died on 14 October 1944, near Ulm, and received a state funeral in order to keep the plot secret.

GERD VON RUNDSTEDT, GERMAN MARSHAL

Born on 12 December 1875, Gerd von Rundstedt took part in the First World War and, after the war ended, continued his war career in the *Reichswehr*, first in the cavalry division and then in the 3rd Berlin division. Opposed to social democracy, he did not support Hitler's national-socialism either. He retired in 1938, but was recalled to the military a year later after Germany declared itself at war. He began as head of the southern army group which participated in the Polish campaign, then, in December 1939, he was appointed as commander of Army Group A, in charge of the campaign in France.

Thanks to the plans to invade France that he made with his

assistant Erich von Manstein (German marshal, 1887-1973), he won the victory that led to the French capitulation in June 1940. He then went to the Eastern Front, where he took the cities of Kiev and Odessa (Ukraine), among others, in the fall of 1941. However, aware of the Russian army's strength and the harshness of winter, he refused to start an attack against Moscow, as stated in the orders given by the Führer, and resigned on 30 November 1941.

Gerd von Rundstedt was then recalled in early 1942 as commander of the western area, and he continued strengthening the Atlantic Wall. He was forced to work with field marshal Erwin Rommel, with whom he strongly disagreed over what to do in the case of Allied landings. Erwin Rommel suggested repelling an attack directly on the beaches, while Gerd von Rundstedt advocated a strategy of inland combat. Following the landing of 6 June 1944 and the German defeat, he advised Hitler to negotiate peace. He was dismissed and replaced by Hans Günther von Kluge (German field marshal, 1882-1944). Recalled to the head of western command in September 1944 after his replacement, suspected of treason, committed suicide, he was at the head of the last great German attack in the Ardennes in December 1944. Defeated by the Allies, he was dismissed once again. He was captured by the Americans, held in a British prisoner camp and charged with war crimes. Due to his heart disease, he was not put on trial and was released in 1949. He died on 24 February 1953 in Hanover.

ANALYSIS OF THE LANDINGS

A DIFFICULT DEPARTURE

At the beginning of June 1944, Operation Neptune seemed to have been compromised. The landing that was scheduled for 5 June due to the good tide and moon conditions necessary for the success of the attack needed to be postponed because a storm struck the channel from 3 June: Dwight D. Eisenhower would not send ships and troops on an impassable sea and into dreadful battle conditions, neither could he order the fleet that was already in place to retreat, as this would mean risking an unduly delay to the attack and being discovered. However, the bad weather, which complicated the landing, did have an unexpected advantage: Marshal Erwin Rommel, although fully aware that a landing near the English Channel was imminent, considered a landing impossible in such conditions. Therefore, he left France for Germany to celebrate his wife's birthday and meet with the Führer.

Finally, considering the calmer weather forecasts, the U.S. General gave the departure order on 5 June, to begin the landing on the night of 5-6 June. A fleet of around 4 000 vessels left the British ports, carrying nearly 290 000 men under the command of Admiral Bertram Home Ramsay (1883-1945). In addition, Admiral Alan Goodrich Kirk (1888-1963) commanded the American Western Task Force, scheduled to land on the beaches of Omaha and Utah, while Admiral Philip Vian (1894-1968) directed the Anglo-French-Canadian Eastern Task Force, which approached the beaches of Sword, Gold and Juno.

Soldiers belonging to the 4th commando.

AIR DEPLOYMENT

While the ships left the English coast, the aviation began
the operations to allow troops and tanks to quickly enter
territories. With these territories being under German
control, the deployment of airborne troops was essential
to take and secure strategic points: roads, bridges, villages,
artillery, batteries, etc. In this context, intensive bombing
allowed them to weaken the enemy forces, and obstruct
and slow down their ascent to the front. The Allies therefore aimed for military targets (batteries and radar stations
threatening the beach landings) and civilian targets (ports,
factories, railways, communication networks to stop the

arrival of reinforcements).

Troops ready to fire at enemy aircrafts.

The parachute landings began in the early hours of 6 June 1944, on the eastern and western flanks of the landing area. Nearly 23 000 men soared through the Normandy sky and over 15 000 tons of bombs were dropped, thanks to a fleet of over 10 000 aircrafts, gliders and bombers. At 12:20am, the bridge of Bénouville located on the Caen canal, which was essential to the exit of the Anglo-Canadian troops from Sword Beach, was taken by British paratroopers (it would later be called Pegasus Bridge in their honor, as their emblem was the winged horse, Pegasus). Although they achieved heroic feats, capturing bridges and roads with speed and efficiency, many lost their lives, not only in the fighting but also because they became trapped by the installations of Erwin Rommel. In addition, some units of the 82nd and 101st American airborne divisions, blown off course by the wind, landed more than 50 kilometers from their target and many of them drowned in the swamps. This scattering of men around Cotentin and Calvados helped to generate some confusion among the German General Staff.

DID YOU KNOW?

John Steele (1912-1969) was an American paratrooper who became famous for his landing on the village church of Saint-Mère-Église. In the dawn of 6 June, as he began his descent, John Steele was hit by a bullet that caused him to lose control of his trajectory. His parachute was caught in the statues that adorned the church tower. He tried to break free, but to no avail. As fighting raged on in the square just below him, he escaped the shooting by playing dead. However, he was captured two hours later by a German soldier and taken prisoner. He escaped a few days later, returned to Britain and resumed his post as a paratrooper. Ever since, a monument representing him has adorned the tower of Saint-Mère-Église.

The hours before dawn on 6 June 1944 were dedicated to

these intensive parachute landings, while the ships approached the beaches. The German contingents based on the Normandy coast were becoming increasingly concerned about these movements. Unconvinced, the General Staff believed it to be a small-scale operation. Therefore, the German General Friedrich Dollman (1882-1944), head of the 7th Army, and field marshal Gerd von Rundstedt did not deem it necessary to mobilize more troops than those already present on the field. Vice Admiral Karl Hoffman, head of Western naval group operations, feared a large-scale invasion. The German forces were quickly reduced, as they were convinced, thanks to the clever disinformation of Operation Fortitude, that the landing would not take place in Normandy. The German army was therefore outnumbered, with only 1 000 planes, which was one tenth of the Allied air force, and only 40 000 soldiers.

THE LANDINGS

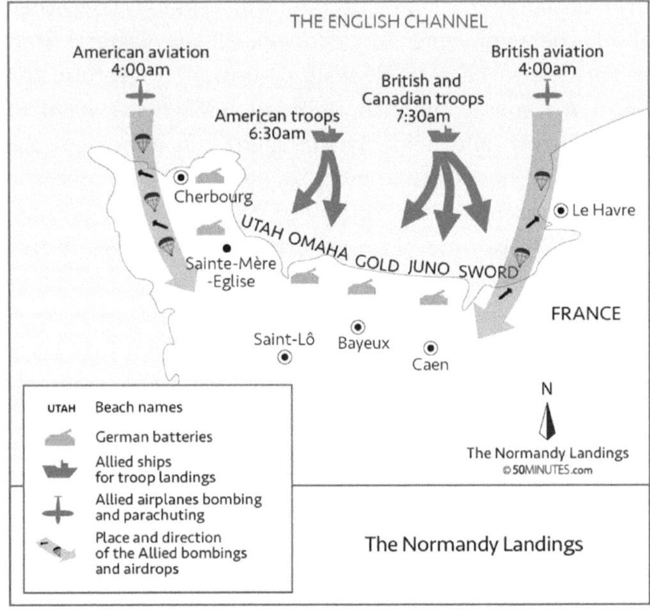

The Normandy Landings

At around 6:30am, American troops landed on the beaches of Utah and Omaha, supported by, among others, amphibious tanks. However, most of them sank due to the rough sea conditions.

One hour later, the British troops approached the beaches of Gold, Juno and Sword. Throughout the morning, men and machines fell on the Normandy beaches under fire from the battleships.

Troops landing on the beach.

On Utah Beach, following a navigational error, the first waves of the attack landed two kilometers away from their target, fortunately docking in a less fortified area. Despite the widely mined terrain and firing from the batteries of Crisbecq and Azeville, the landing on Utah Beach took place as planned and losses did not exceed 200 men (killed, wounded or missing).

At the Pointe du Hoc, the mission of the 225 rangers (special forces of the U.S. Army) was to destroy the batteries overlooking the beach and this cost the lives of 135, even though the German guns had been removed since April.

On Gold Beach, the bombing that destroyed the two batteries of Mont Fleury and Marefontaine allowed for the landing and progression of 25 000 men from the British divisions. At the end of the day, the British, who had lost 400 soldiers, made their junction with the Canadian troops from Juno Beach. The Canadian troops had experienced more difficulties than their Allies. Indeed, adverse weather conditions caused issues with navigation and reefs hidden by the swell of the sea caused losses as soon as the barges landed. Once on the beach, the tide also covered the mines, making them difficult to detect. Of the 21 000 Canadians who stepped onto Juno Beach, more than 1 000 were killed and almost as many were injured or missing. Although they made their junction with the Gold Beach troops, a path still under German control prevented them from liaising with the British troops at Sword Beach.

However, the greatest difficulties were encountered by the 1st and 29th U.S. Infantry Divisions at Omaha Beach, which would be called 'Bloody Beach' a few months later. Preventive bombing failed to overcome the German fortifications there. The beach itself was strewn with mines which were near impossible to neutralize for the military engineers, and the violence of the sea resulted in the loss of most of the amphibious tanks. Added to this was the fact that the German army was present in great numbers that morning for training. The tide also made the shore, littered with corpses and engine carcasses, more and more narrow. It sometimes took several hours for the Americans to progress inland. The toll was heavy: the American losses on that beach were estimated to amount to more than 2 000 men (killed, wounded or missing).

At sea, the warships were also facing mines and bombings by the *Luftwaffe* (German air force) after dark.

THE FIRST STEPS TOWARDS LIBERATION

Once on the beaches, the Allies then needed to conquer the land and seize the towns and villages from the Germans. The first towns to be liberated were those of Sainte-Mère-Église, then Ouistreham and Arromanches-les-Bains.

The 3rd British Division, accompanied by French commandos led by Phillipe Kieffer (1899-1962) and landed on Sword Beach, had the daunting task of annihilating the German defenses and taking the city of Caen, which had been bombed three times that day. But a brief German outburst stopped the capture. Indeed, after a phase of disbelief that delayed their intervention, the German General Staff mobilized its armed forces from 8am. It took time to move these heavy divisions, and they were not operational until early afternoon. Although this largely benefitted the Allies, the arrival of a contingent of the 20th *Panzerdivision* in Caen destroyed the hopes of the British to seize the town before nightfall. It was not recaptured by the Allies until 20 July, after six weeks of heavy fighting that severely damaged the medieval city.

Meanwhile, Marshal Erwin Rommel, who was in Germany, was warned of the catastrophic situation. He immediately left the country without even seeing Adolf Hitler, and returned to France. Furious at the lack of response from Gerd von Rundstedt, and having evidence that he should have kept armored divisions on the coast and not inland, he showed little optimism regarding the events, despite the exhortations of the Führer to resist the onslaught of the Allies.

On the evening of 6 June 1944, approximately 150 000 Allied soldiers landed in Normandy. There were approximately 10 000 casualties, a third of which were deaths. On the German side, the losses were almost identical, although they had three times less men involved. Although the careful preparation and lessons learned from previous landings allowed the Allies to carry out Operation Neptune, it was also due to the flaws of the German device that they were able to reach the Normandy coast. The German submarines, which were poorly equipped, were easily located, facilitating their destruction before they caused too much damage to the Anglo-American fleet. The disagreement between Erwin Rommel and Gerd von Rundstedt over the position of the armored divisions also counted for a lot in the lack of responsiveness of the *Wehrmacht*. Finally, the German officers remained convinced that the Normandy landings were only a diversionary tactic to conceal a larger-scale operation, making them hesitant to respond, for fear of not having enough men left to defend a more strategic location.

DID YOU KNOW?

The landings were covered by fifty film crews, who risked their lives just like the soldiers they accompanied. To ensure the film coverage of the landing, Dwight D. Eisenhower hired Hollywood director George Stevens (1904-1974), who later became famous in the 1950s for his Oscar-winning films *A Place in the Sun* (1951) and

Giant (1956). He directed a team of more than thirty operators responsible for news in the Allied countries and filmed in color. American photographer Robert Capa (1913-1954) was also present, although his shots would be less lucky as the laboratory technicians in charge of their development damaged most of the negatives.

REPERCUSSIONS OF THE LANDINGS

THE BATTLE OF NORMANDY

On the evening of 6 June 1944, Operation Neptune proved to be a success: the human losses were lower than had been expected, despite the failure to seize Caen. However, this was only the first phase of Operation Overlord, whose ultimate goal was to force the German enemy to surrender and end the war. Thus began the Battle of Normandy, with progressive deployment and army landings. Allied surveillance and air bombings continued to fight the German forces and repel them, to continue their progression towards the major cities.

The Allies took advantage of their strengths: already numerically superior, reinforcements of men and material arrived regularly through landing operations on the beaches, but also through the artificial Mulberry harbor B, placed in front of Arromanches, and Mulberry harbor A, in front of Omaha Beach. Each day, nearly 30 000 men, 7 000 vehicles and 30 000 tons of supplies arrived in Normandy. The Pluto pipeline linking England and France under the English Channel provided the fuel needed for the various activities.

On the German side, there were more difficulties in gathering their troops. Arriving dispersed, and not having time to regroup, they were constantly harassed by Allied aircrafts and attacked by the Resistance, the *Panzerdivision* was kept under control by the imposing Allied bridgehead.

The landing of more troops, equipment and especially fuel depended entirely on access to the ports. However, the domination of the Normandy ports was not guaranteed and the Allies had the bitter experience of this during the landing at Dieppe in 1942. Thus, from the fall of 1943, construction began on two official harbors in British shipyards. With over 15 km of floating piers, 33 quays and 600 000 tons of concrete, Mulberry ports A and B were a technical feat. Scheduled to enter service three weeks after the landing, Mulberry A, located in front of Saint-Laurent-sur-Mer, was destroyed by the storm that raged from 19-22 June. Only Mulberry B, located in front of Arromanches, was operational as of 14 June. Vestiges of these installations are still visible along the Normandy coast.

Despite the catastrophic situation and the increasingly significant losses, Adolf Hitler refused the pressing demands from his marshals to retreat and he ordered them to stand up to the enemy. On 12 June, American troops seized Carentan, a strategic point connecting Cotentin and Calvados. That same day, the first German V1 rockets were launched on London and relentlessly bombarded the city. Erwin Rommel, who was not as optimistic as the Führer, tried to organize the defense of Cherbourg, which he knew would be the next target of the Allies – and whose recapture would prove disastrous for the Germans. However, most of the tanks were mobilized to face the British in Caen. U.S.

troops took advantage of this weakness of the German defense to take the port of Cherbourg on 21 June, which they took from the enemy five days later. On 1 July, the Allies took control of the port that could accommodate supply vessels from 17 July (as they needed time to repair the port facilities sabotaged by the Germans), thus backing up Mulberry B.

In Caen, the men of Bernard Law Montgomery sieged the city through an encirclement strategy, but they faced fierce resistance from the Hitler Youth and the SS troops. The high number of casualties (more than 4 000 British died) prompted the halting of the siege maneuver in favor of a final attempt to seize the city. Lacking sufficient artillery, the Allies made use of systematic bombing which destroyed most of the *Luftwaffe* division responsible for protecting the area, the tanks of the 12th *Panzerdivision* and almost all of Caen. On 20 July, the city was retaken by the Allies.

However, despite some successes, the Allied advance was slow, bogged down in the Norman hedgerows and laboriously gaining every meter of ground, first towards the south of Normandy. At the end of July, Coutances and Avranches were seized from the enemy. The troops then went back towards the north, performing an encirclement maneuver of the German troops, cutting off any possibility of retreat and opening the way to the Seine. On 9 August, Le Mans was invested by American soldiers and on 12 August, the men of the 2nd Armored Division of General Philippe Leclerc took Alençon. The Germans were now trapped between the U.S. and French troops in the south, the British in the west and the Canadian and Polish in the north, in a territory of 40 kilometers by 20, known as the Falaise Pocket, located between the towns of Argentan, Vimoutiers and Trun, where fighting raged from 12-21 August. The Allies were victorious, but at the cost of heavy casualties. This was the end of the Battle of Normandy, the Allies then marched towards Germany.

THE PROVENCE LANDINGS AND THE LIBERATION OF PARIS

The German situation was becoming more and more critical. The troops mobilized during the Battle of Normandy retreated to the Seine, and then to Germany and the Netherlands. At the same time, those based in the South of France were facing a new front. In developing Operation Overlord, the Allies also planned Operation Anvil. This involved a landing in Provence, to free the territories of the south-east of France, to take the ports of Marseille and Toulon, and then to go up along the Rhone in order to trap the enemy by making a junction between the armies of Operation Overlord and Operation Anvil. On 15 August 1944, nearly 2 000 ships approached the coast between Toulon and Cannes, supported, as in Normandy, by a deployment of parachutists. In two weeks, Provence was freed.

In Paris, the announcement of the imminent arrival of the Allies in the West and the South led to the mass uprising of the population against the German occupiers, a rebellion which was organized by the Resistance. Being in a perilous situation, the Resistance appealed to Allied troops, who had not yet planned to pass through Paris. General Philippe

Leclerc, supported by Charles de Gaulle, but without the approval of his American superiors, decided to march through the capital. The 2nd Armored Division entered the city on 24 August 1944 and was joined the following day by the 4th Infantry Division, sent as reinforcements by Dwight D. Eisenhower. Paris was finally liberated.

The Allies, whose armies came from Normandy and Provence, performed their junction in early September, then took the direction of Germany.

SUMMARY

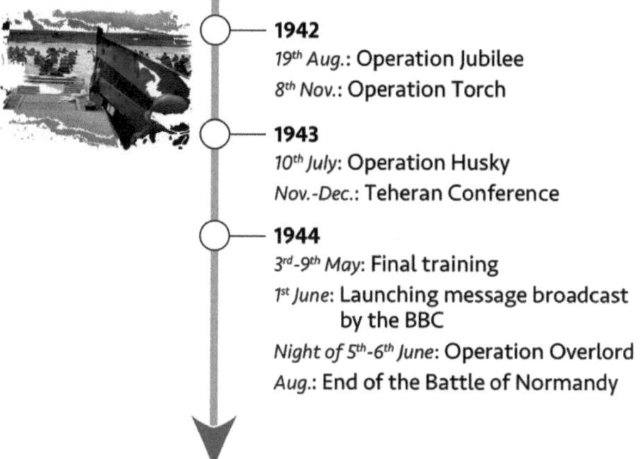

1942
19th Aug.: Operation Jubilee
8th Nov.: Operation Torch

1943
10th July: Operation Husky
Nov.-Dec.: Teheran Conference

1944
3rd-9th May: Final training
1st June: Launching message broadcast by the BBC
Night of 5th-6th June: Operation Overlord
Aug.: End of the Battle of Normandy

- From 1940, the war between the Allies and the Axis took place on the Eastern Front in North Africa, where the Allies organized a landing in 1942 that enabled them to defeat the *Afrikakorps* of Erwin Rommel.
- In 1943, at the Teheran Conference, the 'Big Three' (Britain, the United States and the USSR) agreed on a major plan: Operation Overlord. This plan aimed to finally beat Germany in Europe. The first phase involved landing on the beaches of Normandy, and was scheduled for June 1944.
- On 5 June, Operation Neptune, led by General Dwight D. Eisenhower, was postponed due to bad weather.
- On 6 June, shortly after midnight, the air landings and parachute drops of the Allied forces began.

- At 6:30am, the first tanks and the first Allied troops arrived on the beaches of Normandy.
- 150 000 Allied soldiers managed to land, among which there were 10 000 losses.
- The next step for the Allies was to reclaim the towns and villages occupied by the enemy. First, the municipalities of Sainte-Mère-Église, Ouistreham and Arromanches-les-Bains were released.
- Meanwhile, the 3rd British Division had the heavy task of liberating Caen. But, following the violent German reaction, the Allied troops did not succeed in doing so until 20 July.
- The German army was now cornered between the U.S.-French troops in the south, the British in the west, and the Canadian and Polish troops in the north. In August 1944, the Battle of Normandy came to an end, opening the way to Germany for the Allies.

We want to hear from you!
Leave a comment on your online library
and share your favourite books on social media!

FIND OUT MORE

BIBLIOGRAPHY

- Azéma, J.-P., Paxton, R. and Burrin, P. (2004) *Le 6 juin 1944*. Paris: Perrin.
- Beaupré, N. (2012) *Les grandes guerres. 1914-1945*. Paris: Belin.
- Bournier, I. (2013) *Le débarquement et la bataille de Normandie. Du 6 juin 1944 à la libération de Paris*. Brest: Éditions Ouest-France.
- Kemp, A. (2004) *6 juin 1944. Le débarquement en Normandie*. Paris: Gallimard.
- Lecouturier, Y. and Bournier, I. (2011) *The Beaches of the D-Day Landings*. Brest: Éditions Ouest-France.
- Wievorka, O. (2010) *Normandy: The Landings to the Liberation of Paris*. Trans. Debevoise, M.B. Massachusetts: Harvard University Press.

ADDITIONAL SOURCES

- Bailey, R. (2010) *Forgotten Voices of D-Day: A Powerful New History of the Normandy Landings in the Words of Those Who Were There*. London: Ebury Press.
- Beevor, A. (2014) *D-Day: The Battle for Normandy*. London: Penguin.
- Carell, P. (1998) *Invasion! They're Coming! German Account of the D-Day Landings and the 80 Days' Battle for France*. Pennsylvania: Schiffer Publishing Ltd.
- Official website of the Omaha Beach Memorial Museum <http://www.musee-memorial-omaha.com/en/>

ICONOGRAPHIC SOURCES

- Soldiers belonging to the 4th commando. Royalty-free reproduction picture.
- Troops ready to fire at enemy aircrafts. Royalty-free reproduction picture.
- Troops landing on the beach. Royalty-free reproduction picture.

LITERATURE

- Ambrose, S.E. (2016) *Band of Brothers*. London: Simon and Schuster.
- Burgett, R.D. (2000) *Currahee!: A Screaming Eagle at Normandy*. New York: Dell Publishing Company.
- Perrault, G. (1967) *The Secret of D-Day*. New York: Bantam Books.
- Ryan, C. (1994) *The Longest Day: The Classic Epic of D-Day*. New York: Simon and Schuster.

FILMS, TELEVISION SERIES AND DOCUMENTAIRES

- *The Longest Day*. (1962) [Film]. Ken Annalin. Dir. USA: Darryl F. Zanuck Productions, Inc.
- *Histoires parallèles*. (1994) [Documentary]. Marc Ferro. Dir. France.
- *Saving Private Ryan*. (1998) [Film]. Steven Spielberg. Dir. USA: Amblin Entertainment, Mutual Film Company.
- *Ils ont filmé la guerre en couleur*. (2000) [Documentary]. René-Jean Boyer. Dir. France.

- *Band of Brothers.* (2001) [Television series]. USA: Playtone, DreamWorks Television, HBO.
- *6 juin 1944, ils étaient les premiers.* (2013) [Documentary]. Jean-Michel Vecchiet. Dir. France.

MUSEUMS AND COMMEMORATIVE BUILDINGS

- Normandy American Cemetery and Memorial, Colleville-sur-Mer (France).
- German war cemetery, La Cambe (France).
- Mémorial de Caen (France).
- Le Musée du Débarquement, Arromanches (France).
- Omaha Beach Memorial Museum, Saint-Laurent-sur-Mer (France).
- Memorial Museum of the Battle of Normandy, Bayeux (France).
- Pointe du Hoc (France).
- Bunkers and battleship vestiges, situated along the Normany coast, in Mont Canisy, in Longues-sur-Mer, in Azeville, in Maizy, etc. (France).
- Overlord Museum, Colleville-sur-Mer (France).
- Utah Beach, Musée du Débarquement, Sainte-Marie-du-Mont (France).

IMPROVE YOUR GENERAL KNOWLEDGE

IN A BLINK OF AN EYE !

www.50minutes.com